The Will of Happiness

The Will of Happiness

Dr. François Adja Assemien

Copyright © 2022 by Dr. François Adja Assemien.

All rights reserved. No part of this book may be reproduced in any form or by any electronic or mechanical means, including information storage and retrieval systems, without permission in writing from the author and publisher, except by reviewers, who may quote brief passages in a review.

ISBN: 978-1-959434-49-8 (Paperback Edition)
ISBN: 978-1-959434-50-4 (Hardcover Edition)
ISBN: 978-1-959434-48-1 (E-book Edition)

Book Ordering Information

The Regency Publishers, US
521 5th Ave 17th floor NY, NY10175
Phone Number: (315)537-3088 ext 1007
Email: info@theregencypublishers.com
www.theregencypublishers.com

Printed in the United States of America

Contents

From The Same Author vii
Introduction ix
1 Life And Struggle 1
2 Life And Happiness 4
3 Life And Power 7
4 Power And Happiness 10
5 Happiness And Morals 12
6 Happiness And Law 15
7 Happiness And Religion 17
8 Psychology And Happiness 20
9 Individual And Happiness 23
10 Family And Happiness 26
11 Country And Happiness 29
12 State And Happiness 32
13 Humanity And Happiness 35

Conclusion 39
Book Summary 43
Author's Biography 45

From The Same Author

The Golden Rules for Personal Success, Health, Happiness and Salvation, Handbook, Edilivre, 2016
Introduction to philocure, essay, Edilivre, 2016
Les Rebelles Africains, novel, Edilivre, 2016
The World is worth nothing, essay, Edilivre, 2016
Forbidden Africa, novel, Edilivre, 2016
The Art of Living in America, Edilivre, 2019
President Donald Trump and Africans, essay, 2020
Côte d'Ivoire hurts, essay, Edilivre, 2018
African Consciousness, essay, Edilivre, 2016
Moral and spiritual education, manual, Edilivre, 2016

Thomas Sankara as Thomas More and Socrate, essay, Ouagadougou, 2020
Ahikaba, novel, Mary Bro Foundation Publishing, London, 2018
Côte d'Ivoire and its foreigners, essay, Black Stars, 2002
Political Thought to Save Côte d'Ivoire, Essay, 2003
The African Guide to Philosophy, Human Sciences and Humanism, Abidjan, 1985
Electoral code, novel, Ebav Stars, 1995
Portrait of the good and the bad voter, the good and the bad candidate, essay, Black Stars, 2000

Introduction

This work is not the work of a court judge or of a moralizing and reconciling angel. Rather, it is the work of a philosopher-sociologist. I am a participating observer. As such, I try to describe and explain certain realities of the world (the dualities). I therefore guard myself against moral and value judgments. I make judgments of fact, of objectivity that allow us to understand and know what is happening in the world. I am an agent of knowledge. I am not a lawyer who distributes sanctions to people who behave well or badly in society or who violate the laws and disturb the public order. My sociological investigation and My metaphysical speculation go beyond morality, ethics, legalism, positive law. So this book may shock and hurt some people because it is not complacent. It is philosophy with hammer blows. Nietzsche and Machiavelli, two realistic and truthful philosophers, did it before me. This book fights the prejudices of vulgar men, the lies, the illusions harmful to humanity.

I positivism, vitalism and pragmatic eudemonisms. Wanting the happiness of humanity is not child's play. This is very serious. It is a deadly fight, a tragic act of demolition and reconstruction. The end justifies the means. In great evils, great remedies must be employed. The stake is worth it. The goal is worth tragic action. You are warned and warned. Philosophers and humanists like Karl Marx and Roger Garaudy have warned humanity about the very serious risks and the dangerousness of contemporary Western civilization. They denounced, criticized and legitimately condemned Western practices based on the desire for power, domination, massacre, exploitation of man by man. They denounced the barbaric, warlike, destructive actions of the capitalists (hegemonism, elitism, eugenics, extermination of humanity). Their reading of history is topical and uplifting. It is enlightening, objective and premonitory. The capitalist and hegemonist West is still at work against humanity. It continues to create conflicts, weapons of mass destruction, to provoke genocidal wars. He invented all kinds of poisons to achieve his macabre, apocalyptic goals (covid-19). Thus the UN agenda 21, the depopulation of the earth (Malthusianism, eugenics), the drastic reduction of the world population, the new satanic, Freemasonic world order, the destruction of civilization, the application of charter of imperialism, zombification and control of peoples through compulsory vaccinations. Mr. Emmanuel Macron, President of France, announces the arrival of the Beast (of which the Bible speaks) on earth. He emphatically teaches us that the evil, satanic Beast is present in the world today. Mystics, Freemasons, Illuminati, wizards are hard at work. They are creating chaos (Revelation).

In his humanist works called **Call to the Living, Biography of the 21st Century, the Alternative, Dialogue of Civilizations, The West is an Accident,** Roger Garaudy, the humanist, warned us about the supreme danger posed by the West, the fabricator of nuclear and other weapons. He was a great visionary, a very honest philosopher. He taught us that not only did the West bring nothing significant and positive in the creation of civilization, but it also wants to destroy the world, humanity and all that other peoples have created by its culture. barbarism and materialism. He and Karl Marx did not believe in saying so. And here we are today. The fact is there. It is patent. It is before our eyes. These two visionaries are right. What to do now? Satanists, demons and Luciferians hold the whole world in their hands. They are actually creating their new satanic world order. Humanity is in danger of death. All human beings will be controlled, mistreated, persecuted, oppressed and exterminated if they do not defend themselves. Humans will lose all of their fundamental rights of freedom, life, justice, sovereignty, happiness, health, security, peace, dignity, independence, self-determination, the enjoyment of our property and of our personal and national wealth.

Luciferian vampires, capitalists, globalists, predators, imperialists, terrorists, slavers and colonialists will alienate us, enslave us, rob us and kill us. This is their program and their avowed intentions. Forewarned is forearmed. He must be on his guard. He must defend himself valiantly. He must go on the offensive-defensive. It is the legitimate Damocles complex. Who wants peace prepares for war. He is obliged to wage a just, legitimate war. It is compulsory and saving self-defense. Let us avoid the ostrich policy, cowardice, imbecility. Let us have the common sense, the intelligence, the courage to confront and defeat the global criminals, cynics, dictators, wherever they are found. Let's take them to court, to prison... Let's save humanity, civilization, morality, ethics, law by all means. Let us engage in a battle of total responsibility, of liberation, of the restoration of our dignity, of our sovereignty, of peace, of security and of global salvation. Let us not be resigned to the supreme danger, to the fierce, murderous and merciless offensive of the enemy. This is insane, silly and irresponsible. No one has the right to take our lives with impunity, to impose his diabolical ideas, his counter-values, his anti-values, his Luciferian, satanic paradigms, his unhealthy vision of the world, his macabre ideology on others. Let us put an imperative, urgent and absolutely end to this by our bravery, our valor and our courage. Its a question of life or death. The situation is serious. Let's change the course of history in our favor. Roll on universal freedom, peace, security, justice and fraternity! Long live universal love! Long live the equality of peoples and races!

1

Life And Struggle

What is life? Life is how much time we spend on earth and how we spend it. This time contains our actions and their consequences, that is to say the work and the struggle. These are conflicts, wars, violence, power struggles, power exercises, pleasures, joys, pains, sufferings, happiness, misfortune. It's all called history. History is the sum of human experiences. She aims for happiness. The conquest of happiness is an imperative duty for the living. It manifests itself in the struggle. And the struggle (combat) is the expression of strength, of power. It consists in attacking others and defending oneself in order to achieve happiness, that is to say power, the ability to exist, to be good.

Life is the dynamic sum of our actions. These actions aim to bring us happiness, that is to say to make us powerful. **Happiness is the exercise of power**. And the power is exerted against the others, that is to say the men, the animals, the plants, nature, the universe. It is the struggle. It consists of wars, conflicts, domination, slavery, colonization, imperialism, oppression, exploitation of man by man, predation, massacres, genocides. It is imposed on humanity as a duty. It's like a right, a good. It is a general law, an absolute imperative. To live is to act, to struggle, to fight, to conquer, to dominate, to be happy or to disappear from the earth. Hard law but law. This is the reality that has existed in the world for millennia, since humanity was born. It is happening in Africa, Europe, America, Asia, Oceania. It is unmistakable and inevitable. Nothing could prohibit or prevent this. The hypocrisy of men which is expressed through ascetic morality, law, religion and humanism cannot suppress it. It is a futile attempt. This is fatal. Everything that man does points in this direction. The condemnations, the speculations, the religious, moral, legal and philosophical dogmas are vain and powerless in the face of history. The story mocks royally this.

Such is the nature of men, of peoples and of the destiny of the world. It is the duty to live and the will to happiness. This is relentless. Nietzsche understood this well. He says it brilliantly in **The Will to Power, in The European Nihilism, in Thus Spoke Zarathustra, in The Genealogy of Morals and Par-de là le bien et le mal**. He was called a berserk and a cynic. But, in truth, it is not. He is simply realistic and objective. He is a truthful, honest and responsible thinker. Honor and glory to him. He is convincing. He sided with the masters, the aristocrats, the birds of prey and the blond beasts against the bleating lambs, the slaves, the decadent, the weak. He is the opposite of Karl Marx who defends the proletarians, the weak he wants to replace the masters, the powerful by organizing them, raising awareness and pushing them to revolutionary action. Finally, he understood that living requires power, strength, that struggle is the engine of happiness, the central pillar of life. He thus joins Nietzsche. Everything alive is a wrestler. He must struggle to be happy. To be happy is to be powerful. It is to be strong. It is to dominate, use, alienate, objectify, exploit others (men, animals, plants, minerals, water, gas). Each individual, each family, each country, each tribe, each continent and each race are in this race, in this dynamic. Geopolitics accounts for this. We use all the means for this company: morality, law, religion, politics, army, police, justice, school, economy, ideology, philosophy, science, technology, art …

These are all the means employed to struggle, to live and to be happy. The end of life is happiness. And happiness is power, that is, domination over others. History and psychology teach us this. All the living are in struggle against each other. You do it or you perish. This struggle is carried out individually or by team, association, group (family, nation, state, people, clan, race, continent). It consists in working, in assaulting, in submitting, in using others. We are all enemies among ourselves as the living desiring happiness, power. Friendship works in this direction. Fraternity and love of neighbor serve this same fundamental cause. Marriage between man and woman, family, nation, conventions, national and international institutions obey this dynamic, this universal law: the struggle for happiness-power.

2

Life And Happiness

Every living being wants to be happy. Happiness is the common goal of all living things. It puts all living things in competition, in competition, in struggle against each other. The law of the jungle is the main law of life. It is universal law. It is natural, human, animal. This is the reason of the strongest. Everyone wants to live. It means everyone wants happiness. What is happiness? Happiness is what fundamentally or best defines every living being. Its modes of expression in humans are pride, pride, self-love, well-being, feelings of power, assurance, serenity, superiority, ease, convenience. The one who is happy manifests his states of mind. He puts himself above the vulgar qualities that ascetic morality teaches us. These vulgar qualities generally translate the negation of the will to live. Thus littleness, weakness, renouncing power, strength, violence, evil, humility, obedience, submission, pity, love of neighbor, self-denial, giving self, compassion, empathy ... The happy man is located beyond good and evil, according to Nietzsche (**Genealogy of Morality, Beyond Good and Evil**). He practices the morality of masters, aristocrats, dominators, that is to say tragic morality. He despises feelings of pity, fear, shame, love of neighbor, regret, kindness, generosity, compassion, affection and humility.

The Will of Happiness

The happy man is a ruthless warrior, a victor. He is without remorse, without faith or law. His law is the law of the strongest. Adolf Hitler, Napoleon Bonaparte and César Borgia embody the virtues of happy men in history. They manifested the aristocratic ideal exalted by Nietzsche. What does the identification of life with happiness mean? It means that life involves struggle and power. Life is the deployment of force, of destructive, creative, innovative, renovating energy. This energy is both physical and mental and works against others. It makes it possible to dominate, to subdue, to use others as a means, instrument, object, thing. These are the facts that make up history. This can be seen everywhere. Let's look around us and our own daily lot. We are all more or less dominated, exploited, instrumentalised and objectified. Whether we are a political leader, worker, employee, man in the street, employee, employer, we all suffer from servitude, submission, domination, sociological, psychological, theological, metaphysical and historical burdens. We are not always aware of it because it is not always visible, objective or material. Among men there are the blind, the deaf and the dumb.

Life is dynamism, transforming energy hence progress, evolution, historical development. The living is always active, offensive, aggressive, combative. As such, he is sometimes victor and sometimes vanquished. It is always in the making, in motion. Its nature is neither completed nor closed. He is sometimes a master and sometimes a slave, and the cycle of victories and defeats continues indefinitely. No victory is final. No defeat is final. The king can become a beggar and the beggar can become a king. At each moment, man must reinvent himself in order to stay alive or to disappear. So humanity perpetuates itself indefinitely in time and space. Thus it reproduces, multiplies, develops and makes progress. It destroys and rebuilds itself. It sinks into the indestructible, inexhaustible and infinite Great Whole. Thus the universe, nature and the world preserve beings as enemy brothers. The struggle is general. It is the war of all against all. It uses the means or weapons that are morality, law, religion, politics, economy, science, technology, art, ideology , philosophy etc. Men are necessarily drawn into and maintained in this vital struggle without ever being able to put an end to it. It is fatal.

3

Life And Power

What is the relationship between life and power or between living things and power? Life is an endless struggle. The living is an unrepentant, inveterate and irreducible wrestler. He was born a wrestler. The struggle is its primary nature. This is its essence. Every living person is a natural warrior. To live is necessarily to fight against others to satisfy one's needs of all kinds. It is to conquer the means of its development, of its well-being. It is to create the conditions for its security, its comfort, its success, its prosperity, its wealth, its power, its influence, its glory, its honor, its dignity. Thus we are perpetually in struggle, in war, in competition, in competition with the others (family members, comrades, colleagues, classmates, compatriots etc.). It does not stop until death. And death is our ultimate failure, our ultimate defeat. It's a catastrophe. He who is dead is definitely and absolutely defeated. He is eliminated from the race for happiness, power, domination. He lacked strength, power.

Power keeps us alive, in struggle, and weakness destroys us, makes us lose every chance of winning the battle for life. Power is the expression of life as a creative, renovating, innovative energy. The essence of life is power. Who says power, says creativity, inventiveness, domination, authority, activity. The living is opposed to weakness. He wields power as a wrestler, warrior, fighter. He does this physically, mentally and verbally. Power is the main attribute of the fighter, the wrestler, the warrior that is the living. This is its basic virtue. Without this, he is not a dignified living, a normal, responsible, efficient wrestler. He will be defeated very easily by his adversaries, his competitors or his enemies. Any living person or wrestler absolutely needs power. It is his primary tool or his main weapon. Power is a quality or a vital virtue. This is very beneficial. Power is physical, mental, social, spiritual, moral, political, economic, financial, intellectual, military, sexual. It is good for everyone. So the wife needs a powerful husband, the child needs powerful parents, a nation needs a powerful army and soldiers, powerful citizens. Power creates happiness, security, peace, prosperity, wealth, progress, public and individual salvation.

There could be no life possible without power as a cardinal virtue. Beware of the individual or the people who despise or condemn power. This is fatal. Life is an act of power in its details because it is a phenomenon of struggle. A helpless wrestler is easy prey, resigned prey. He is not worthy of life. He is an inconsistent and ashamed living. Life selects beings by all kinds of trials, by its law of power, its law of the jungle, its law of the strongest. In the dynamic of struggle, the strong survive, persist in their being, while the weak perish, disappear. This is valid both biologically (Charles Darwin) and sociologically. This is how we must understand pragmatic vitalism, aristocratic and voluntarist morality (Nietzsche), the morality of responsibility and commitment (Jean-Paul Sartre) and Marxian morality advocating the revolutionary violence of the proletarians. The will to power and the struggle for happiness are peculiar to the living being. These are two sacred laws of the universe, of nature and of civil society. No one can escape it. This is why there are conflicts, injustices, violence everywhere, within families, nations, continents, all over the world and between these entities. That is why everyone is everyone's enemy. Men are against men, animals and plants. Animals are against people, animals, plants (the food chain). Hatred and love of neighbor enter into this dynamic of universal conflict and struggle for happiness and power. The manifestations of charity, affection, compassion, empathy, kindness, generosity, kindness very badly veil the fundamental reality, egoism, the wickedness of beings. These are hypocritical gestures, strategies and traps. It is deception, bad faith. It can be unconscious. All so-called humanitarian acts are suspect. These are dangerous ploys. Let us beware of all of this. Let us be vigilant and careful. All gifts and favors are poisoned. It is the expression of the will for power, for domination. It is the veiled evil, the aggression camouflaged by hypocrisy, dishonesty, deceitful cunning.

4

Power And Happiness

What is the relationship between power and happiness? These two things are practically synonymous. Nietzsche and Karl Marx will not tell us the opposite. Power makes happiness. Happiness is the enjoyment of power. It is the expression of power. Power involves struggle, combat and victory. It is the success, prosperity, security, peace, freedom, autonomy, sovereignty of an individual or a people. For example, if Africans want happiness, they must make themselves powerful, that is to say, be free, independent, sovereign, decolonized, disalienated, emancipated. They must fight and do everything to be safe, at peace. They must be able to dispose of their property, their wealth, their country, their life. They must fight against their tormentors, their predators, slavers and colonizers. They must achieve victory over their imperialist enemies of all time. It is called the liberation war or the popular revolution. These are the acts of power (the will to power). They must change the course of history and transform their collective lot. Such heroic behavior confers happiness. Happiness is therefore the result, the consequence of power. It is the victory gained over the enemy or the adversary.

Americans, for example, are happy. How and why? They fought against the British settlers. They defeated them. They are no longer colonized, dominated, exploited, possessed by the English imperialists. They are liberated, independent, sovereign, at peace and united. They are a worthy, brave and responsible people. They also fought against Indians or natives. They made themselves masters and owners of the land they called America. They have won all their struggles, taken up all their challenges. They have formed themselves into a higher, feared, irresistible power. America is the world's leading power in almost all areas (economy, army, technology, science, culture, art, sport…). So no other nation in the world can dare to provoke them, threaten them, challenge them, attack them, wage war on them. They are the strongest and therefore the happiest. They are the policemen of the world. These are the conditions and the proofs of power and happiness.

If the Africans (or the antitheses of the Americans) , fight and act in this way they too will undoubtedly be powerful and happy. The way to happiness is open to everyone. It is enough to have two powerful feet to walk and pass. Happiness is torn away after a hard fight. It is conquered by military, intellectual and mental power. It is built by heroic effort, iron discipline, revolution, voluntarism, bravery. It is the fruit of dynamic, constructive action and thought. All the natural and human assets are present in Africa. What do Africans lack in order to be happy? It is the will to power, courage, union, solidarity, bravery, intelligence, popular struggle, revolution, patriotism, the desire for freedom and happiness. To want is to can. To want freedom is to act and struggle to be free. Wanting happiness is also acting and struggling to be happy. In short, a powerful and revolutionary people are always free, at peace and happy.

5

Happiness And Morals

What is the relationship between happiness and morality? Are these two things compatible? We have already said that happiness is the result of power, that is, victory over the enemy or the adversary. All living things are in a power struggle. They are all fighting against each other. They are enemies, adversaries, competitors, rivals. It happens everywhere, in every family, in every village, in every country, in every department, etc. The common goal of all beings is happiness. Everyone uses all the means given to him to try to achieve this goal. Some methods are effective while others are not. Here we judge the moral. Further on, we will also talk about other means such as religion and positive law.

Morality is a special teaching applied to the living. It speaks to our mind and tells us what to do and what is forbidden to us by society as a whole. It shows us what is good and what is bad from the point of view of society. It judges our behavior. It authorizes some and condemns others. It shows us what is good and what is bad. It is present in the detail of our daily life. She guides us everywhere. It is on all our paths. It administers our relationship with ourselves and with others. It acts in the interest of society and the individual. It represents the voice of society and of our conscience or Reason. It speaks to our minds and intelligence at all times. She has psychological power. It is the invisible authority which censures us, blames us or congratulates us according to the quality of our action. We are all his slaves. It regulates, controls our life. She has been guiding us since our childhood. It has filled our minds with prejudices and dogmas. It imposed on us choices, tastes, feelings, ascetic ideals coming from religion, opinion and philosophy (ethics of Kant, Spinoza, Aristotle). The Christian religion, for example, translates it into ten commandments called the **Ten Commandments of God** : "Thou shalt not steal", "Thou shalt not kill", "Thou shalt not commit adultery", "Thou shalt not bear witness lie against your neighbor "," You will not covet anything that is your neighbor "," You will honor your father and your mother "… Kant's ethics, or morality of duty, reinforce this with categorical imperatives. For example, "Act so that you treat humanity always as an end and never simply as a means", "Act as if the maxim of your action should be set up by your will in universal law of nature".

The morality thus presented displays the negation of the will to live. She denies the struggle and therefore the happiness. It is opposed to power as a principle or condition of happiness. We are faced with two categories of morality: ascetic morality (Christian and Kantian) and the tragic or aristocratic morality of Nietzsche (realist philosopher or philosopher of the body). Christian and Kantian morals deny reality, life and happiness as well as the means to achieve happiness. They are enemies of the living, mercilessly engaged in the fight for happiness on earth. This fight forbids illusion, prejudices and superstitious beliefs. The end imposes its means on us. Machiavelli understood this by giving effective and salutary rules to political leaders in **The Prince**. He thus inaugurated, founded political science. Like him, Nietzsche, positivist or realist philosopher, demolished metaphysical, theological illusions and the prejudices of vulgar, Christian, ascetic morality. These two thinkers are right. Indeed, life is precious. Very valuable. We must not sacrifice it to the wind. It takes place on earth and not elsewhere. We cannot save humanity and the world which are endangered with illusions, prejudices, lies, hypocrisy, intellectual dishonesty. We are at war and we need victory. It is with absolutely effective weapons that we will be able to win this ruthless war. Thus tragic or aristocratic morality which advocates power, pragmatic and vitalist voluntarism is preferable.

6

Happiness And Law

What is the relationship between happiness and positive law? Are these two things compatible? The conquest of happiness is called the struggle. It divides people. It pits them against each other (conflict, war of interest, violence). So we are all enemies. Man is a wolf for man (Thomas Hobbes) in the name of the interest and happiness which are the common ends of all living. The happiness of a people or an individual consists in the enjoyment of physical, social, economic, financial, material, military, political, mental, intellectual, spiritual, cultural power. It is obtained through fierce struggle, work, fierce combat. Thus happiness is opposed to ascetic morality. What about positive law (legal laws)? Law is based on morality. It serves as an objective, concrete instrument of morality (positivism). It is its expression, its physical, material manifestation (police, court, judges, prison). While moral laws are liberal, non-binding, legal laws are, for their part, very rigorous, binding, coercive. They physically and materially sanction beings. They inflict corporal punishments: arrests, imprisonments, bans, homicides or the death penalty, etc. They limit expression, freedom, action and prevent the struggle for happiness. They slow down the manifestations of individual and collective power. They make people small, weak, powerless. They cut off the arms and feet of men to prevent them from fully acting. The law thus makes war on war, on warriors, on wrestlers seeking power and therefore happiness.

From this point of view, the law is dangerous, harmful, illegitimate. He is the enemy of the living. He is at the service of the masters, the dominators, the enemies of the people, the popular masses. It is a weapon manufactured by the strongest, the powerful to defend themselves, to protect their goods and their interests. It is charged with barbaric, unjust, illegitimate violence against the weak. Thus the State with its police, its army, its court judges persecutes, oppresses, represses the wrestlers, the fighters for life and happiness. It takes away human freedom and the right to life, to happiness, to power. Legal laws are made by the strong for the strong and against the weak. They reflect the desire for power, domination, predation, exploitation, oppression. It is unfair. But through the cunning, demagoguery and Machiavellianism of the state, these laws are presented to us as instruments of peace, security, equality, liberty, justice, brotherhood, union, discipline and happiness for all. What a grotesque lie! What an illusion! This teaching is criminal against the people, the weak.

The republic, democracy and the state are thus devoid of any legitimacy. The laws are discriminatory, liberticidal, genocidal, imperialist, slavery, colonialists. For example, Colbert's Code Noir, the Charter of Imperialism, the Colonial Pact imposed on Africans by General de Gaulle, Apartheid in South Africa, the UN, NATO, the European Union, 'African Union etc. The search for happiness through positive law (national constitutions that can be manipulated at will) is an illusion, a scam, a swindle, a hypocrisy, a crime against humanity. The state is fundamentally Machiavellian and criminal. He is dishonest, unfair. It is a trap against the people, the weak, the fighters, the living. Legality (State) is against legitimacy (people). The will to power, to happiness of the weak (the struggle) is opposed to the positive right of those in power. It is thwarted, torpedoed by the cunning, demagoguery, hypocrisy and Machiavellianism of powerful criminals, predators.

7

Happiness And Religion

In the previous chapters, we have defined happiness. We have put it in a conflicting relationship with ascetic morality and positive law. We have defended and saved it from the mortal danger of ascetic morality and positive law. Let us continue this same salutary work here with religion. Happiness is in the struggle. Better still, it is obtained through ruthless struggle as a manifestation of life. To live is to struggle and to want happiness. It is at the same time wanting all-out power. The happy being is the one who exercises the power making him free, independent, sovereign, prosperous and putting him in peace. A happy being is master of himself. He is autonomous. He is not conditioned or alienated by forces external to him. It is not dominated, exploited, enslaved, colonized. He has his life, his goods and his wealth of all kinds (material, physical, economic, social, financial, intellectual, cultural…). He is fully and strongly himself. He is powerful and formidable.

Religion is a teaching and a practice which conveys dogmas, prejudices, superstitions, emotions, illusions, lies, myths. If it takes hold of man, it breaks him, neutralizes him, paralyzes him, weakens him. It intoxicates him, alienates him, transforms him into a sheep, a donkey, a fool, a docile slave. She said to him: "Happy are those who are poor in spirit, gullible, submissive". "Happy are those who believe without seeing". "Happy are those who renounce life, goods and material, earthly riches, happiness". "Happy are those who leave the world for the beyond of life, for the afterlife". "If someone slaps you on the right cheek, you have to stretch out the left cheek." Religion turns man into a zombie, a mental patient, a delusional dreamer who can end up dying very poor, miserable and unhappy. The believer in God is disgusted with life and the world. He dreams of heavenly Paradise, of the kingdom of God. He doesn't like the world. He hates, despises, condemns life. He hates himself. He is ashamed of himself as a man.

He learned that he is very dirty, wicked, sinful, unworthy, and destined for Hell. He condemns power and life. Religion is the negation of the will to live and of humanity by means of lies, myths, prejudices, illusions (God, soul, paradise, hell, angel, bliss, beatitude, eternal life, kingdom of heaven, holiness , Holy Spirit).

Religious practice consists in preparing for death, for the afterlife, for the beyond of the world where the believer can meet God, the angels, the holy spirit. The believer wants to unite with God, to identify with him (yoga in Sanskrit). Therefore, he is indifferent to our world below, to its realities and its problems. He is not of the world, even if he is, despite everything, still in the world insofar as he is alive. He finds it useless and stupid that others continue to struggle, to claim the right to live, earthly happiness and power.

Now it has been proven that it is the clerics associated with businessmen, governments, bogus scientists, owners of pharmaceutical companies, big capitalists, mystics, wizards of all stripes thirsty for human blood who are in demand. destroying civilization, the world and slaughtering humanity with impunity. They are the globalists, the eugenics, the utopians, the satanists, the devils, the demons, the racists who are creating a new world order by the extermination of the peoples of the earth. This macabre project has been recorded in their so-called holy or sacred books (Bible: apocalypse) for millennia. It is taking shape nowadays. This is evidenced by the bacteriological and virological warfare unleashed over the entire surface of the earth at the same time from 2020 (covid-19). It ruthlessly ravages humanity. It is the greatest genocide or the greatest crime against humanity in history. It is bio-terrorism never known before. This is the UN agenda which plans to depopulate the earth (Agenda 21), killing 90% of the world population and the remaining zombifiant with poisons and toxic vaccines, deadly s , anti- natalist . It is the work of a world government which is being put in place in an accelerated fashion. This collectivist and authoritarian world government imposes on us the satanic order of the Beast (apocalypse). Will humanity allow itself to be done until the end? Wait and see. Good to hear, hello! Forewarned is forearmed. He is doubly on his guard. Its a question of life or death. Man only lives once. It is enough to say.

8

Psychology And Happiness

What is the relationship between psychology and happiness? Psychology is at the forefront of the human sciences. We can summarize it by the Socratic formula which says: "Know thyself". Socrates invites man to study and know himself as a human being. The other Greek philosophers before him rather studied nature, the universe. They were physicists, naturalists, cosmologists. They answered the question: what is everything made of (what is the matrix of the world)? For Thales of Miletus, it is water. For Heraclitus of Ephesus, it is fire, heat, energy. For Empedocles, it is love, the opposite of which is hatred. For Pythagoras of Samos, it is the number. The study of man as an object of knowledge (soul or spirit) appeared for the first time in Socrates, humanist and psychologist. For him, it is absolutely important for man to know his nature, the functioning of his mind, his vocation, his destiny. Indeed, psychology makes it possible to understand and explain human reactions, emotions, feelings and human behavior or behavior. For Socrates, knowing oneself as a spirit or a soul is the basis of moral life and happiness. Socrates' concern is moral. It is about cultivating moral virtue in order to be happy. What matters most to Socrates, a great moralist, is good. The idea of good is for him the supreme idea. It is mother virtue.

Ignorance of moral virtue is the cause of evils and misfortunes. Our soul is initially predisposed to do good and nothing but good, never harm. Man is naturally good. He is not mean. If he happens to do harm, it is because he was mistaken about the nature of the good. Evil is involuntary. It happens out of ignorance or by mistake. No one is wicked on purpose. The role of philosophers and kings is to guide vulgar men towards good as a divinity located in the **intelligible world** (realm of Ideas, of intelligence). Socrates calls this journey to the intelligible world the dialectical ascent. The duty of scholars or philosophers is to get vulgar, ignorant people out of obscurantism, from **the sensitive world.** They must take them out of the dark cave (world of sensations, beliefs, conjectures, prejudices, lies) where they have been locked up like prisoners since their birth (the myth of the cave). He who is enlightened for having contemplated the Idea of Good is virtuous. He is not passionate. He is guided only by Reason. He is happy. He becomes king and educator of passionate ignorant people. The philosopher is king or the king is a philosopher. This is the condition or the responsibility of intellectual and political elites around the world.

The common man, the vulgar man, is moved, dominated by opinion, prejudices, illusions, deceptive appearances, beliefs, passions, sensation (sensitive world). Psychology is indeed an effective discipline in the struggle of the living for happiness. It is a science of domination because it teaches the secrets, the laws of the human mind. The individual who holds these laws can become powerful and the master of others. Philosophers-psychologists transform the minds of men, strengthen them, enlighten them on themselves, on their condition or situation. They are spiritual, mental guides. Thus Nicolas Machiavelli, author of **The Prince,** is the intellectual guide of the governors, of the politicians. Nietzsche is another and not the least. His greatest disciple or hero is Adolf Hitler, a great Nazi fighter. Karl Marx is the spiritual son of Hegel, author of **The Phenomenology of the Spirit.** (the dialectic of master and slave). All these thinkers give us rules of life that illuminate the struggle for happiness. Karl Marx formed a plethora of wrestlers who made themselves masters of humanity: Lenin, Mao Tse Toung, Fidel Castro… Lenin created and led the Union of Socialist, Soviet Republics (USSR), Mao created and led the Great People's China, Communist. Fidel Castro created and led the Communist Society of Cuba until his death. The followers of these thinkers can no longer be counted in the world. They are present on all continents. They upset the order of the world and transformed history. They overthrew the bourgeois capitalist regimes in most countries in Europe, Asia, Africa and America. All this proves that psychology makes masters and heroes in the struggle for happiness. Thomas Hobbes also did this work in **Levianthan** (man is a wolf for man) . In the struggle for happiness, one must acquire power with the thinkers, the sages who teach the truth and explain the reality. We must listen to the philosophers of history, realistic philosophers, objectives. We must flee from liars who teach illusions, moral prejudices as well as ascetic priests. These poison and weaken our minds. They keep us in obscurantism, ignorance, submission, servitude, powerlessness .

We need the strength, the power, the pugnacity to live in our societies which are jungles. To live is to seek happiness. To seek happiness is to fight against others. It is to be strong, powerful in the jungle world of wolves and lions. If you are a sheep among hungry wolves and lions, do all you can to save your head. All men are enemies. There is no real, natural fraternity, friendship, love of neighbor, charity, philanthropy. These things are deceptive and harmful ascetic ideals, illusions and moral and religious prejudices (mortification) . We must avoid being a victim. Observe the daily reality in your life. Let yourself be guided by this. It is beneficial. It is practical, vital psychology.

9

Individual And Happiness

The individual who lives is in struggle. Her life is a constant struggle which is expressed through her daily activities. He is not passive. He's pretty active. His actions compete with the actions of others (family members, work colleagues, men in the street…). All living defend themselves against each other and attack each other . Man is a wolf to man. Brothers, sisters, fathers, mothers, wives, husbands, cousins, cousins, uncles, aunts… are in constant rivalry, in competition. It can be in the form of open or underhanded conflict, hypocritical, camouflaged in friendly, fraternal appearances, with words and gestures of kindness, generosity, compassion, solidarity, affection, empathy, of charity, altruism, self-sacrifice. Jealousy, hatred, selfishness, wickedness are often concealed behind the angelic, humanistic and divine appearance. Herein lies the very dangerous trap which easily catches naïve people who let their guard down or lack vigilance. So they let themselves be surprised by their hidden enemies and they regret their imprudence and their stupid trust in others. Know that no one wants to see you succeed, be happy, powerful. Life is a deadly race for all to happiness, glory, honors, pleasures, power, the top, or the throne. Life is a merciless general struggle. The strongest crush, eliminate, slaughter the weak.

Everyone is ready to destroy you quickly, fail to make you or steal your success, your happiness, your victory, your possessions to be happy as long as possible (even if it is so illusory) .Telle is reality. It is a universal constant. Everyone wants to kill you, destroy you and take your place in the race for happiness if you are in the lead somewhere. Watch out if you are ahead of the others, if you are about to win a race, to win a victory. All bad moves are good against you and are allowed in this competition. The end justifies the means. This is valid in all areas and everywhere: at work, at games, in public, political, artistic, social, sporting, economic, family, national, international life. Everyone wants to satisfy his pride, his vanity, by proving to everyone that he is the strongest, the most powerful, the best. Everyone wants to submit, to dominate everyone. It is then the war of all against all. But this is carefully veiled by diplomatic manners, that is, hypocritical, deceptive and deceptive. The struggle for life and happiness is very real. It takes on very varied, diverse and subtle complex shapes, proportions and dimensions that are hidden in the small details of life. It can be violent, overt or gentle, discreet, veiled. If you are attentive, intelligent, you will discover it in the words or in the actions of others. How many people or families have they not poisoned, sacrificed or murdered theirs out of jealousy, hatred, envy, competitive spirit, rivalry, selfishness, egocentricity, wickedness?

The struggle for life, happiness and power is elsewhere called the instinct of life or instinct of self-preservation. It often proceeds by trickery. Sometimes it is frontal, brutal, without veil, direct. It can be conscious or unconscious. It depends on the characters and temperaments of men. People are different from each other. So this struggle manifests itself either by finesse, gentleness, cunning, hypocrisy, courtesy, politeness, kindness or by brutality, violence, wickedness, cruelty, barbarism, cynicism, savagery . Are you looking for your personal happiness? The others are also looking for theirs. So you inevitably meet on the same path that leads to happiness. It means that you are using the same means that are available to everyone. Each acts to the detriment of each. Everyone attacks everyone by snatching this or that. Hence the eternal conflicts of interest, power, happiness, no one. We never do good for good, for free, voluntarily, out of charity, altruism, selflessness. For love of neighbor or of mankind. Divine love does not exist. We do good out of interest, pride, vanity, constraint, with the intention of gaining something. Usually it is to dominate others, to humiliate others and to display their proud and conceited power. The beneficiary of the benefit is in a weak position. It is pitiful. It looks like a bird that has lost both wings and can no longer fly. Such a bird is nailed to the ground and awaits the help of a savior. He is quite helpless. He is no longer worth anything. He is no longer a bird. He is no longer a wrestler. He lost the right to life. He is at everyone's mercy. He is easy prey; everyone has the right to death or life over him. So it is with a lion with all its fangs and claws torn off. This lion has fallen into absolute helplessness. It is reduced to its simplest expression. The struggle for life, happiness and power is over for the bird without wings and for the lion without fangs and claws. These two beings are defeated or dead.

10

Family And Happiness

The family is the digest or the summary of the whole society. It is a micro-state, a micro-country or a fraction of humanity. At its head, there is a chief (the father of the family) and at its base, there are the people (the mother of the family and the children). It is a coherent group, well structured and oriented towards a collective goal of the happiness of all. Each element of this group is a conqueror, a wrestler desiring happiness. He wants to enjoy, enjoy maximum of puissanc e and the collective economy. Each member wants to be powerful, to grab the wealth, the treasure, the goods and the common patrimony. It's a fierce struggle, a tight competition, without mercy. We are talking about palaver, a war of inheritance. Children fight among themselves, driven by the will for power and happiness. They are enemies. The father and the mother are also in struggle for the same reason of happiness, of power. It is the conflict of interest, power and generalized happiness, the war of all against all. Within families, we find the conflictual situation of the global society or of humanity. There are dominators and dominated, masters and slaves, lions and sheep. Everyone defends himself as best he can. He wants to save his skin, his head, his interests. It can cause death.

The will to happiness is the will to power, the will to superiority and interest. The whole constitutes life as a field of violence, struggle, conflict. Morality, law and religion are used for these bellicose, hegemonic, historical ends. They are weapons, instruments that light, maintain, feed the fire (division, conflict). They fan embers and flames, revive them. In a given family, each has its adversaries, its competitors, its rivals and its enemies. There is no family in which one does not encounter manifestations of jealousy, hatred, envy, animosity, selfishness, wickedness. But these mental viruses necessarily sow tension, violence, evil. But this can sometimes be veiled by a deceptive appearance of peace, harmony, security, love, affection, brotherhood, solidarity, union, discipline, justice, equality of condition. , friendliness, humanity. Man is always a wolf to man in all situations and in all positions. He is not and never will be an angel, a holy spirit, a god. It is not made in the image of God as it is said. C is rather the man who created human beings in his image he calls Satan, demon, devil, lucifer. He curses them hypocritically and places them in heaven or elsewhere. Man uses all of this in his struggle and his race for happiness, power and domination.

Here we present the true face and the true role of the family. We must not be mistaken about the family. We must not idealize it, crystallize it. We must not lie by taking the family for what it is not. We must not play the game of moralists, religious who crystallize the family by attributing to it ascetic virtues that it does not have. The family is not heaven on earth. It's a basket of crabs, a jungle. Let's not hide this from the world. We are not the ones who want it or make it that way. But it is naturally as such. To present it otherwise or under angelic, divine colors and appearances is to be in bad faith. We say what things are and not what things should be. This is our mission. We fight prejudices, lies, illusions, superstitions, false beliefs, myths and appearances that are deceptive and harmful to man. Only scientific truth and objectivity can save humanity. The realism and objectivity that characterize our words are not signs of pessimism or cynicism. Far from it. The end justifies the means. If you want happiness, use the appropriate, necessary, effective means (the truth). Don't do the opposite. Don't take the wrong route. Don't be fooled. The right road here is science, psychology, that is, knowledge of the human mind. Know yourself and study others.

11

Country And Happiness

A country is the land of struggles for the happiness of each and everyone. This is where all the rivalries, all the competitions, and all the deadly competitions take place. This is the biggest jungle where there are lions, sheep, grasses, gazelles, elephants, snakes, all beings, all the scariest, most dreadful, most dangerous things. There takes place the war of all against all in the name of power and happiness. It is up to everyone to acquire the necessary strength to stand up to others and be happy. If man was born free as it is said, everywhere he is in chains (Rousseau). He is in a fierce battle against the irons, that is to say obstacles, constraints, dangers of all kinds, competitors or adversaries. His country subjects him to endless trials, challenges and difficulties. So to survive, the individual must be educated and succeed in school. He must study and cross several levels in his school education. He is obliged to obtain diplomas, degrees and professional qualifications. He must be well trained in order to deserve a job, a salary. It is subject to examinations and selective competitions. It's a struggle, a fierce competition. It is merciless. We want the learner to be strong, intelligent, brilliant, ingenious, talented, courageous. The chances of success are given to the best, the most deserving.

We choose the champions, the elites (elitism). The weak, the mediocre and the shabby are eliminated, thrown in the trash. Their life is mortgaged, threatened, in danger. They are unwanted. They constitute the waste of society. They are unworthy, ashamed. They are condemned to vegetate, to live on, to remain in precariousness, indigence, misery, suffering, poverty, on the margins of society. They lead a despicable underground life. Some unfortunate people manage to turn the tide, meet challenges, heroically climb the ladder of life and reach the rank of masters, nobles, champions. Because the will to power and happiness lives in them despite everything. Their pride is whipped. And they are making a glorious place for themselves in society. They avenge their past failures and defeats. They overcome their handicaps, their weaknesses, their deficiencies. They glean victories, conquer laurels, palms of gold. They are legendary. They immortalize themselves. People who are favored by fate, by birth, have it easier. They were born already kings or masters. They are endowed, at birth, with all the material and financial means for their social, economic, political and intellectual ascension. Their success is guaranteed by the power and happiness of their wealthy parents. Everything was done for them before they were born. They enjoy the inheritance, the patrimony of their family. They are profiteers, the lucky ones. They are well born. They are born in abundance or glut. They no longer have to struggle. They have happiness as a gift. It is their gift from God. The others are obliged to build their own happiness. They have the duty to fight for power, to become masters and kings. This is how the son of a poor person, of a citizen of the lower social class, becomes President of the Republic or a very high executive of a country. This case is frequent in the world. History shows it to us in Africa, America, Europe, Asia and Oceania (artists, athletes, politicians, scientists, philosophers, writers). They are deserving, talented, competent, brave, brave. They are heroes. They have won their struggles and their salaries with the sweat of their brow. They are the most worthy and the most respectable.

The Will of Happiness

The country is at the same time a jungle, a basket of crabs, a hell and a paradise. You can do what you want with it. You must benefit from it as much as possible. You have to get the most out of it. It gives you a lot of opponents and areas of struggle to build you up and make you happy. If you are strong, wise, you will legitimately profit from it. You will be powerful, happy. You will be a master, a hero, a genius, an elite. It all depends on your will, your courage, your intelligence, your wisdom. Your personality will do the rest, your destiny and history. You can transform your country, enlarge it, make it richer, more powerful, more beautiful or, on the contrary, destroy it, put it in decline. The future and the future of the world, societies and peoples always depend on the will of a few individuals. History shows it to us. Look around you, in your country, and elsewhere, in the world. You will see heroes, sages, geniuses who rule and dominate the world. You have to be inspired by them. Their cases can strengthen you, straighten you up and make you progress. It can guide you to glory, honor, greatness, happiness, and salvation. Be a good example for humanity. Be a school for others like certain celebrities or historical legends whose works challenge us by their exemplarity and their beauty. Humanity always needs heroes, masters, geniuses, wise men to lead it to glory, to power, to happiness. Be the strongest, the smartest, the richest, the most powerful, the biggest, the happiest. You must use your Reason and your will. Everything is possible for man. At valiant heart nothing impossible. You have to have the rage to conquer and win all your battles. Be like the lion. You should never give up a noble, useful and interesting fight. It will bring you to glory. To be conquered without peril, one triumphs without glory (Pierre Corneille).

12

State And Happiness

The state is the supreme political institution for each country. It translates concretely into the government with all its structures and functional institutions. It represents the symbol of absolute domination. The anarchists fight it because of its sovereign functions of repression, coercion, enslavement, subjugation and alienation of men. It is seen by them as the supreme danger against individual life and liberty, against the will to power and happiness. The state is the direction of civil society. It is endowed with several structures and institutions through which it manifests its authority and power over men. He is the seat and the creator of laws. Obedience to laws is either servitude or freedom. Freedom is the right and permission to act or not to act granted to citizens by the state . We have a duty to obey only the just, legitimate and salutary laws of the State and not the arbitrary, cynical, sadistic, criminal laws of men, be they Presidents or kings . The state is a moral phenomenon (Hegel). It is not a leviathan, a monster devouring men, freedoms and goods of all. The State wants to be the engine of the promotion and the safeguard of peace, freedom, security, order and happiness of the citizens. He must treat men as free beings and citizens but not as things, objects, slaves, animals. Its laws are considered as the expression of the general or popular will, that is to say the common good (in a democratic and republican framework). This therefore excludes arbitrariness, autocracy, bloodthirsty dictatorship (in the African manner), barbarism, injustice, contempt for the dignity of the human person (ascetic and religious morality, morality of Kant's duty).

We must ask ourselves whether the historic states are legitimate, responsible, whether they meet the requirements of the moral definition of the state. The despotic, tyrannical, absolutist and totalitarian practices of today's countries are the opposite of the notion of the state. There is no real democracy, republic, popular consensus, freedom, egalitarian justice, respect for citizens' rights (right to life, right to dignity, right to happiness, right to freedom, right to health, right to power…) in the world, in this era of corona virus (covid-19). All the current political, social, health and economic decisions of the rulers of the world are immoral, inhuman and criminal towards the peoples (the formation of a new satanic, diabolical, Luciferian world order with its share of unbearable and unacceptable misfortunes) . It is the height of arbitrariness, totalitarianism, wickedness and cynicism never seen on earth. These are crimes against humanity and murderous, genocidal follies on a planetary scale such as bio-terrorism or bacteriological warfare (covid-19, AIDS, EBOLA), eugenics, the creation of a world government collectivist, the extermination or drastic reduction of the world population, the depopulation of the earth thanks to science, technology, medicine (abnormal, illegitimate, anti-scientific vaccines, biology, war and all kinds of cruelties and unimaginable follies.

Today's world states are illegitimate and dangerous. It is saying little. They are cold monsters. They lie and coldly murder their people. They are driving their people to the slaughterhouse. They slaughter them like sacrificial sheep. The satanic covid-19 (bio-terrorism) of globalists and Malthusianists is a very acute global moral crisis. How can men be mean, cruel and criminal up to this point? The last straw is that they are not bothered or punished. They blithely taunt everyone and enjoy absolute impunity. What world are we in? And despite all that, we still dare to talk to us about justice, equality, peace, security, happiness, democracy, republic, freedom !? Who are we laughing at? We don't give a damn about the mouths of sheep. It's easy and risk-free. But we can not laugh at the mouths of lions. The people must understand this. As long as they remain sheep, such will always be their fate on earth. The current states do not make us happy but rather our misfortune. They deceive us, manipulate us and gleefully massacre us. Laws are made by the Mafia for the criminal interests of the Mafia. They are made by the strong against the weak and the people. Democracy is a blatant lie, a dangerous myth, a childish illusion, a deception. "If there were a people of gods, they would govern themselves democratically; such a perfect government does not suit men, "says Jean-Jacques Rousseau. Men are passionate, selfish, unjust and wicked. Historic states are jungles and baskets of crabs. The rulers are hungry wolves and lions in front of the sheep peoples. They have a right of life or death over the flocks of sheep. They put everyone's life in danger. They offer us the Apocalypse and the Beast today. French President Emmanuel Macron, a great globalist and Freemason, tells us openly on television: "We are at war. The enemy is invisible. The Beast is there. Our time is living this. We are experiencing it ". He was talking about covid-19 to the French people. He thus announced the arrival of the disease which he happily offers to France and to the world (the new world order of Freemasons, Illuminati, mystics, wizards, satanists and demons) . People of the earth, wake up! Open your eyes, react, defend yourself, before it's too late. More than ever, the hour is too serious. We are all in danger. Let's talk and take action. Let's resist. Defend, protect life, civilization and humanity such as nature, the universe and the great Whole gave it to us. Let us all together reject the new world order and all its sterilizing and deadly poisons. Let's prevent the demons from controlling, directing, zombifying, animalizing, robotizing and ultimately exterminating us.

13

Humanity And Happiness

Humanity is at the same time the sum, the quality and the value of men. There are about eight billion people on earth. For millennia, people have lived together in the world. They are in all kinds of relationship. They have forged complex and endless links between them. They organized themselves into nations, tribes, clans, republics, kingdoms, villages, towns, families etc. This is in accordance with their nature. Men have organized themselves in this way out of interest, in order to achieve happiness. Unity is strength. It is good for individual and collective security, peace and power. The great human family has formidable enemies in the world. These are natural forces or disasters and other dangerous beings such as animals. However, the various human groups mentioned above regularly clash with each other. They do not coexist peacefully, fraternally, convivially, harmoniously. Living together is difficult and often compromised by the faults of human nature. So interest, egoism, egocentricity, tribalism, clanism, regionalism, racism, jealousy, greed, greed, the will to power and happiness. So love of neighbor, perfect union, discipline, justice, equality, solidarity, compassion and mutual aid do not really, necessarily exist.

Men are divided and are in struggle, in conflict and at war with each other out of interest, by the desire for power, domination and happiness. The war of all against all results in civility, patriotism, nationalism, regionalism, ascetic morality. Consciousness of one's ego, one's family, one's village, one's town, one's nation, one's tribe, one's clan, one's race is problematic. This is a source of conflict, violence, injustice, wickedness, aggression, war (imperialism, slavery, colonialism). The desire for power, domination, interest, personal and collective happiness causes catastrophes and genocides. Thus egos enter into war (egoism), families enter into war (familialism) , nations enter into war (nationalism), homelands enter into war (patriotism), tribes enter into war (tribalism), clans enter into war (clanism), ethnic groups go to war (ethnism-ethnocentrism), races go to war (racism). Finally, there are more reasons or factors of division, violence and conflict between men than there are to unite them, save them and build them collective and individual happiness. Everywhere, we see endogenous and exogenous struggles and conflicts (struggle of classes, groups, races, societies, continents).

In short, humanity is against humanity. All living are enemies, competitors. Hostility is present everywhere in the human family. Love of neighbor is selfish, selfish, violent. Goodness is paradoxically filled with wickedness. Kindness, generosity, compassion, charity, altruism and philanthropy are in truth their opposites. It's a game of hypocrisy. Even renunciators, ascetics, Puritans, saints, yogis are selfish and wicked. They are in the dynamics of evil. They are wisely selfish. There are two kinds of selfishness. There is the selfishness of the vulgar man and the selfishness of the wise man . The Dalai Lama advises men to practice selfishness in wisdom. It consists of veiling the unavoidable cynicism, cruelty, wickedness. This is hypocrisy. The religion of compassion and empathy is a school of hypocrisy. Self-sacrifice, self-denial, self-giving, surrender, renunciation, detachment as well as all other ascetic ideals are therefore dangers to life. It is the negation of the will to live. These are attempts to suppress life as a violent and tragic phenomenon (Nietzsche's pragmatic vitalism). Because life is always expressed as a desire for power, for happiness, struggle and tragedy. Life is selfishness and violence. This is undeniable. You cannot change the nature of men. Wanting to transform men into God, into Buddhas, is to kill them, to remove them from the earth. Saints do not exist in this world. Those who are called saints are actors and pranksters. Rather, they are world champions when it comes to the struggle for dominance, power and happiness. They are tragedians, fighters for life with their own methods (ascetic ideals as a strategy of revenge and resentment). They are outstanding warriors. They are unmatched, very cunning. Such is their merit as deniers of life. To deny life is to affirm it even more, by other means. To fight for power is to seek power from infinite power. To condemn humanity is still to praise, magnify and glorify humanity. It is trying to do an impossible thing. Humanity heroically resists and survives all moral and religious condemnations inspired by resentment and the spirit of vengeance. To fight happiness is to desire it more. To praise weakness, helplessness, littleness, compassion, pity, charity, self-giving, kindness, love of neighbor, is to deny them in an absolute way. It is to condemn them without appeal, with more wickedness, firmness and harshness. These are the human paradoxes. This must be taken as an apodictic truth.

Conclusion

The will of happiness. This is the title of this work. The will is an operative and regulating concept. Happiness is too. These two concepts enclose primordial values. From their dialectical relation, we have shown the dialectic that there is between life, power and struggle. We have built a fundamental and critical teaching on these notions to enlighten vulgar men and dogmatic minds. Our concern is not to moralize humanity. Because we do not consider this enterprise useful or fruitful. We work more as an agent of knowledge. We are aiming for material and historical truth. We have set aside moral, ascetic and religious prejudices as the opium of the peoples in order to open the way to the knowledge of life and of man as Nietzsche did before us (pragmatic vitalism). For us, true, objective knowledge is the supreme value. It is priceless. It is she who can help and save humanity in rout, in confusion and in decay. Socrates said: "Know thyself". The objective and passionless knowledge of man by man is an absolute and primordial necessity. Efficient, rational and salutary morals, law and politics can flow from this. The good education of mankind must be based on this. It is the study of mental life, behavior, the human spirit. It's called **psychology.**

The laws discovered by psychologists are very precious to those who struggle, who want to make their way and walk towards happiness or build a good and great personality. Thus psychology represents the mother science and the engine of individual and collective life, of political and economic life. Life is based on struggle. It is a warlike act. To wage war and win it, it is necessary to have effective weapons. The best weapon here is a very good knowledge of the enemy, his weapons, his strategy and his tactics. Psychology plays this role in our daily struggle for happiness and power. Psychology teaches us that man is defined by the will to power and happiness. And the will to power elevates man to greatness and happiness. It makes the individual a master, a dominator. It gives it freedom, peace, security. Men and peoples who lack the will to power are enslaved by the powerful. They are reduced to animals and objects. They are controlled, dominated, colonized and subjugated by peoples who manifest the will for power and happiness. This is the operational value of the will to power and to happiness.

So Africans are enslaved and colonized by Europeans and Orientals because they lack the will for power and happiness. They don't struggle. They behave like sheep in front of lions (conquerors, predators) that are other peoples. They are cowardly, fearful, weak, unable to defend themselves. Whoever is incapable of defending himself, of fighting, loses his life, his freedom, his sovereignty, his goods, his wealth. He does not have peace, security, happiness, dignity. He naturally undergoes the law of the strongest, the most powerful, the most armed. It happened to Africans who suffered from slavery and colonization. The world is a jungle. Everywhere it is the relation of force, relation of dominator to dominated, of master to slave. There is no friendship, pity, brotherhood, love of neighbor, kindness, generosity, compassion of the strong and the powerful for the weak, the aboulics, the sick. Between peoples, there is no love, friendship, brotherhood. There are only interests to defend (General de Gaulle sic). It's a predator-to-victim relationship. The lion does not negotiate with its prey. He does not seek permission from it before devouring it. Only his strength does everything for him. She assures him of his victories and his happiness. It is the power alone that saves sentient beings in this world. It is therefore necessary that each individual

The Will of Happiness

and each people who aspire to happiness cultivate strength and power. Whoever wants peace prepares for war. The one who wants freedom, sovereignty, greatness, prosperity, happiness as well. War is just for whom it is necessary (Machiavelli). It is the war that made all the great and beautiful nations of this world. There are wars of liberation, conquest, invasion, occupation, colonization, independence, sovereignty. This is the dynamic of life. This is the history of the world. Africa has not yet understood this fundamental and primary law. She accepts her subordination to the West and the East. She does not refuse this historic evil. She cheerfully assumes it at her expense. It still applies the charter of western imperialism and the colonial pact of General de Gaulle. She has just accepted even covid-19 and its deadly, eugenic, sterilizing false vaccines. (genetical therapy). Such is his latest stupidity and his last supreme scandal to date. Its corrupt, alienated and subjugated elites (intellectuals and politicians) very actively help the capitalist businessmen, the globalists, the eugenics, the negrophobic racists, the Freemasons, the Satanists, the Illuminati, to destroy it, to massacre its populations, to loot, to steal its wealth and its natural and mineral resources.

Book Summary

This book is a mirror, an adviser, a critical guide for all. It allows man to discover man . Moreover, it allows the living being to know the nature, the general purpose and the value of life. If man is looking for happiness, he does not always really know what happiness is or how to find it. He needs a tool for that. Such is the preoccupation of this iconoclastic book. The will to happiness is a viaticum for all the fighters for life, happiness and power.

Author's Biography

Dr François Adja Assemien was born on March 15, 1954 in Côted'Ivoire. He studied classical letters, social sciences and philosophy. A graduate in philosophy (state doctorate) and sociology (license), he devoted ed to the philosophy of education at the university ed, to search academic and in writing. He speaks and e crit three living languages are French, English and German.

He is author of several books published in Europe and America (novels, essays, stories, parts theater). It é also created several concepts such as Afrocratisme the Philocure the Sidarologie, African Consciousness, the Aboubou music.... It is also an artist musician, singer, songwriter, guitarist.

He lives in the United States of America .

www.ingramcontent.com/pod-product-compliance
Lightning Source LLC
LaVergne TN
LVHW040201080526
838202LV00042B/3274